POWER & STATE

I0781699

Lucy Nalangu

James Sawers

*Professor Lucy Nalangu, PhD, CBE

**Some of the things mentioned in this book have to do with current events, the outcomes of which have yet to be determined, as of date of publishing.

This Fine Book Belongs To:

<u>Books of poetry by James Sawers</u>

<u>Nothing Series:</u>

Nothing Works 2nd ED
Meditations on Aikido,
Buddhism, the Tao, Zen, and
other inconsequential things...
Nothing Special: Vol II
Nothing Matters: Vol III
Nothing Exists; Vol IV
Nothing Flows Vol. V

<u>War Series:</u>

Words of War 2nd ed.
Warm Beer Is Not Cool
Go Tell the Crows
Common Blood
Military Maxims*
Military Maxims II*
The Hard Way
(Upcoming)

<u>Color Series: 2nd ed.</u>

Red
Lust Is a Monster
Poems of Life, Love, and Loss

Green
The Other Monster

Blue
The Indigo Moments of Life

Politics

Trumpets -
Poetic Observations on a Presidency
Are You a Nutjob?
The Cockwomble President
American Judgement*
In Search of Value*
Power & State*
FUBAR*
(Upcoming)

Life Series/Standalone

In the Shadows of the Ordinary
Too Deep for Tears
Rainy Nights in Chicago
Silent Love
She Wears the Wind
Accidental Gods
The Colors of Time
Strange Thoughts
Cold Warmth
Kitchen Sink Poetry
Olympus Mons or Bust!
Whispers
Scottish Haiku
Shared Thoughts
Obvious Thoughts
One Life
Just South of Midnight
Broken Things

Humanity Interstellar Series

Humanity Interstellar
The Way of the Vessel*
The Way of the Vessel II*
Humanity Interstellar II
(Upcoming)

<u>Religion/Mysticism</u>

War of Swords
Book of Unwisdom - Conversing in Silence
The Singularity of Being
Full When Empty
Way of Nothingness*

Non-Poetry

White Rose Productions

Nothing-Werks, Inc.
nothingwerks42@gmail.com

Power & State

First Printing June, 2024
ISBN: 9798326412034

My Power

My power is my hate
My power is my love
My power is my humanity
I stand before the greatest gods
In all my weakness
In all my strength
And I know it is not enough
I may fall, but I will not kneel
I will not yield
My final defiance, my final power
Can only be my laughter

~ Elizabeth Rutherglen

*The theology of totalitarianism
always requires human sacrifice.*

~ Prof. James Darwin

WHITE ROSE

*The white rose has many meanings and is symbolic of numerous things. In politics, white roses are a symbol of peace. The image of a white rose is found throughout this book.

In Germany, a non-violent group of students who opposed Adolf Hitler called themselves *"die Weiße Rose"* or *"the white rose."* The name stood for youth and pure intentions. They were captured and two leaders, siblings, Hans and Sophie Scholl, were executed; in fact, beheaded by the Nazis.

Tolerance becomes a crime when applied to evil.
~ Thomas Mann

*One of the most cowardly things ordinary
people do is to shut their eyes to facts.*
~ C.S. Lewis

Political power grows out of the barrel of a gun.
~ Mao Zedong

*Wealth aggregates and becomes political power.
Simple as that.*
~ Daniel Suarez

To limit money is to limit political power.
~ Stefan Molyneux

*Political power does not rest with those who cast votes;
political power rests with those who count votes.*
~ Joseph Stalin

The object of power is power.
~ George Orwell

*Power is a utility. It needs a guiding hand to be useful.
An off/on switch would be helpful, too.*
~ Charles Braeside

*If democracy depends on an educated,
informed citizenry, then democracy is in trouble.*
~ Tristan Graeme Ash

*The ignorance of one voter in a democracy
impairs the security of all.*
~ John F. Kennedy

Contents

Power & State

OVERVIEW

Lucy Nalangu is a Professor of Law, History & Moral Philosophy, PhD, CBE. She is a teacher, writer, social activist, social scientist, and political philosopher, formerly Professor of Law, History & Moral Philosophy at the University of Nairobi, previously taught at the University of Oxford, UK, and at Harvard University, US. Currently, she is a freelance researcher, professional writer, commentator, and consultant.

This volume is a compilation (with permission) of her thoughts, opinions, and ideas, extracted from her published works, her unpublished manuscripts, and personal conversations.

As with Alexis de Tocqueville, almost two centuries before her, Professor Nalangu brings an outsider view on the happenings in the United States, perhaps more objective than native-born.

She also shares the same belief of Tocqueville, that the ongoing movement toward democracy in the West, and perhaps the entire world, is one of the greatest overriding themes in history.

That the drive towards equality for all is one of the most important political and social ideas human civilization has brought forth.

She understands and celebrates the sometimes-sensitive balance that can occur between liberty and equality, the individual, and the community-at-large.

She believes that Democracy cannot be taken for granted, but must be fought for and protected for the value it brings to Humanity and to its future promise.

But there needs to be a constant reminder, that the power of the State, in a Democracy, is derived from the people. Many times, this is so easy to forget, by the State as well as by the people.

The writings herein attempt to straddle the line between the concrete mundane, offering opinions, insights, and possible courses of practical, realistic appraisal and action applicable to the here-and-now, to a type of philosophical speculation that tries to avoid extravagant overstatement.

Words with an asterisk* after them will be found in the DEFINITION section at the back of the book, along with others that may help in understanding the context in which certain words are used.

While Europe's eye is fix'd on mighty things,

The fate of empires and the fall of kings;

While quacks of State must each produce his plan,

And even children lisp the Rights of Man;

Amid this mighty fuss just let me mention,

The Rights of Woman merit some attention.

~ Robert Burns

QUOTES & NOTES

⚙ *In theory, once a political party, and its members, gain power, they should automatically relinquish their allegiance to any one party. True, the party was elected to accomplish certain favored party goals, but the party should now turn its allegiance to the State*, as it now represents all the people, not just its own voters and supporters. In practice, this is rarely done.*

⚙ *'My loyalty is my loyalty' is the new catchword of Trump's party and his supporters. It is based on nothing, as is the party itself, except a drive for power. Any articulated party agenda or program, is seen as superfluous and an actual hinderance to speed of movement, and a limit to their 'free' speech.*

⊛ *The fact that Trump and his party do not have any real political agenda should tell anyone who is paying attention that their only goal is to take power. The only ideology they have and believe in (Christian fascism, aside), is the ideology of bullshit and lies, the more outrageous the better.*

A rational lie can be argued with, can be disputed, but radicalized hyperbole, unburdened by balanced thought and common sense, is just left hanging, untouched and untouchable by rational, logical minds, taking on a life of its own, the truth left far behind. Rinse and repeat, rinse and repeat.... Loudly...

⊛ *Justice is a form of mercy. Justice takes the place of blind judgement.*

✸ *The 'State*' should not be seen as some sort of mystical, distant, entity beyond the reach of mortal men. The State is a construct, created to achieve a purpose, created to achieve collective goals. Created by people. The State, therefore, serves the people. To believe otherwise is to live in an unreal world where individual power is relinquished to the machinery of State control, and people become powerless cogs.*

✸ *It must be recognized that there are people in this world that will stop at nothing to get their way. This can be readily seen all over the world. However, this recognition seems to get more difficult close to home. 'It cannot happen here', is usually, belatedly, recognized as not true.*

✸ *In a two-party system of government, each party, however much they may disagree with each other, however much they may actually hate each other, must recognize the relative importance each party represents to the nation as a whole.*

Neither party wants to totally destroy the other. If this were to happen, dictatorial rule is not far behind. For regardless of any good intentions of the one surviving party, power not used is power lost.

Therefore, without the checks and balances offered by a two-party system, it cannot be relied upon for people in power, to do the right thing all the time.

✸ *In any society, freedom of thought and opinion are meaningless if what is thought changes nothing.*

🌞 *The State, to survive, must provide effective services addressing the needs of the people and the nation as a whole, not just separate party or individual interests.*

Party interests must not supersede those of the nation. Occasionally, there may be an overlap of interests, as a party pursues its particular agenda, but the State, to survive must come before party, must come first.

🌞 *Those who blindly put their self and party above the State are following an ideology, not a form of rational, effective governance.*

✸ *Many people take for granted their basic human rights, their basic legal rights, their basic civil rights, but they should not, for they need to understand that those rights are predicated on the most basic right of all,* which is *the right to have rights.*

This basic right is absent for millions of people all over the world, leaving them without protection and in a limbo from which there seems little recourse, or any great interest in remedying.

✸ *When people have no legal rights, hence no protections, it is not long before someone decides that they have no right to live.*

⊛ *The* rights *of a citizen are legally different from general human rights. Within this distinction the citizen is protected inside a legal framework.*

General human rights are talked and written about, but a clear definition remains unclear.

In the meantime, millions of people, non-citizens, remain stateless and homeless, with no legal protections beyond a vague hope that no one will harm them in the territories they may have landed. Their only 'crime' being what they are, not what they have done.

⊛ *In a recognized 'league of nations', full sovereignty is recognized as not being absolute. Certain rights, duties, obligations are seen as 'international' in scope.*

America has to recognize that there are some people who feel so lost, feel so disenfranchised from what current society offers, or does not offer them, that they demand change at any price, even the total destruction and dissolution of all democratic governmental systems and institutions.

If they see a candidate who offers a way to do this, they will gravitate in that direction. For they see the status quo holding them back and down.

Fear, anger, and hatred demands its removal. They do not care how this removal gets done. In fact, many would prefer to do it violently.

People should not run for public office just in the hopes of manifesting their own personal needs. Public office is a public trust, serving the public good.

☀ *Once a 'hated state' is destroyed, removed, leaving a vacuum in its place to be filled, the ideologists of destruction can now stop pretending that they are a movement of the people, take over the remnants of the state, and using any methods whatsoever, including violence and murder, impose their ideological will.*

☀ *In a thriving democracy*, the people should not see the State as an entity, as a system, beyond human reach and understanding, where they have no power, no influence, or control over it. This leads to apathy and indifference.*

❋ *Citizens have the right and duty to criticize their government and its policies if they think there is a need. Blindly following governmental policies is not patriotism. A citizen has an obligation to help navigate the ship of state. The citizen is, after all, a passenger, sometimes crew.*

❋ *Patriotism should not be blind devotion and obedience to a manmade construct, like the State. A deluded self-oblivion, sacrificing rational thought, individual identity, can in no way be seen as a public good; or, even, a good for the individual citizen.*

⚙ *In theory, Law is above Power. Paradoxically, this is what gives Law its own power. It allows for an impartiality. It is this impartiality that allows Law to impart its will on society as a whole, and be accepted as an unbiassed arbiter, even on the most powerful. In theory.*

⚙ *The threat of 'denaturalization' of some American citizens by the current GOP presidential candidate can be used as a measure of the degree of totalitarian* infection in this party.*

◉ *The chief difference between the Democratic and Republican parties is that the Republican party is made up of individuals who joined this party in order to protect their private interests, or those of their friends and supporters, from government 'interference'.*

The Democratic party is made up of individuals who are willing to act in concert to achieve some public good via some sort of government action.

One party sees government as the problem, the other sees government as a tool to help solve problems that are beyond the scope of individuals to solve alone.

◉ *In difficult times, it is so easy to fall back to a parental role and mindset: 'Just do it! Don't ask any questions!' (or else! is implied). This can be deadly to a democracy. Power gained in this way is difficult to relinquish.*

✹ *While immigration at the American southern border is a major and current issue, and despite fractious dissent and debate over blame and how to manage the massive influx of immigrants, legal and illegal, it must be recognized by all, that immigration is a serious matter, especially mass immigration. Climate change can only make it worse. Uncontrolled, unregulated mass migration can have a destabilizing effect on any nation-state, no matter how strong it is. Ignoring this, not having a uniform national policy on this, created by all sides of the debate, can bring on the disintegration of a country.*

✹ *In a two-party system of government, there must be a mingling of, a sharing of, at least some party interests, even if only just national in scope. Otherwise, a losing party may see its loss more like being vanquished in a war by an alien and ideological enemy, and then may resist its loss of station and power.*

⚛ *Be aware of, and wary of, movements vs parties. They are not the same. The party works within a system. In fact, a party is an integral part of the system itself. The party has a stake in the survival of the State it is a part of.*

A movement can be national or trans-national – and usually is trans-national. Its loyalties are not to a particular country or nation-state, but to its own ideology. It would feel no qualms in betraying its own country if that betrayal would further its own needs and goals. Ideology first and foremost, that is its the path to power.

⚛ *In a Democracy, if all Rights devolve to the individual, the individual must then have a means to protect those Rights if the Law cannot or refuses to do so, otherwise those Rights become meaningless.*

In the United States, the need for a comprehensive immigration policy is a must. If not done, the southern border, especially, becomes more like a police state, where border agents begin to make up their own rules and 'laws' because none are forthcoming from the State. If left too long, this situation can metastasize to the rest of the country. The Law must mean something. But at the very least, to mean something, it must first exist.

Unless an individual takes conscious control of the Law of Process, he will be swept away by unknown forces, relegated to the possible highs and lows of a fate not of his own making or choosing.

✸ *If immigration and immigrants are to work long-term for the good of the nation, and not just provide a momentary, periodic, financial boost, the immigrants need to feel that they have a long-term interest and stake in the wellbeing of the country within they reside.*

Also, immigrants need to be recognized for the short-term and long-term benefits they provide and be given appropriate status and a clear path to full enfranchisement. A country can only benefit from this.

✸ *When creating legal documents, particularly when codifying such concepts, what is 'right' and what is 'good' needs to be clearly defined. One definition may not agree with the other, otherwise. In fact, they may contradict each other at some level.*

✺ *The United States, must be very careful not to create a permanent class of non-citizens, where the path to full citizenship is not spelled out and made achievable.*

Having a permanent underclass of people living alongside fully recognized citizens, can have a corrosive effect, and is not heathy for the State, not to mention the individuals so classified. There is a certain critical level where that unhealthiness can slip into violence.

✺ *Poverty and strife create their own kinship.*

✺ *It was discovered long ago that definite goals and political platforms were not really needed by a political party if they just catered to the tribal longing of some people for a mythical past, or some hoped for idealized future, that they long for, and appeal to a general mood of dissatisfaction. Vague generalities and promises become the operating methodology, as long as people hear what they want to hear.*

✺ *Listen to the language of the mob. Do not disregard it, for the mob* speaks its truth, and its truth will certainly be different from yours.*

❂ *There is a movement within the Republican Party to support Trump and other candidates like him. This movement has no actual political agenda. Its only agenda is to achieve power, and with this power use the machinery of the State to push their own private interests. In fact, this movement is not actually 'Republican'. It spans all political ideologies that it deems useful. Currently, the Republican Party conveniently carries its water, but it could be any party or person who fits its needs.*

❂ *Times of peace and prosperity are anathema to those who seek power for power's sake. Therefore, they seek to unbalance the* status quo *by whatever means necessary. They seek to create movement, for within movement lies the possibility of chaos, and therefore, opportunity.*

❋ *Despite the toxicity of the current Republican party, and the impetus and desire in some quarters to have such a party destroyed, this is not a good idea. True, the current Republican party is proving itself anathema to democracy, trying, it seems, to do its best to destroy American democracy and install some kind of autocracy.*

However, a two-party system is required to protect democracy. It is so much easier for a one-party government to turn into a one-party dictatorship. We cannot rely on the good will and intentions of people to avoid this fate. There must be the counter balance of at least one other party, fighting for its own selfish interests, with the unintentional side effect of protecting the democratic system as a whole.

❋ *Total control of a State requires almost total destruction of the State. The totalitarian leader(s) do not care. Their only limiting concern might be that their country may now appear weak and vulnerable to outside potential enemies.*

✺ *Are Universal Human Rights* only an abstraction, with no basis in history, fact, or inheritance? Currently, any meaningful Universal Human Rights, however formulated, seems to be derived from nationhood.*

We see all over the world those stateless, homeless, populations that are so obviously without rights of any kind just because they are stateless. No State claims them or wants them. Their numbers are too large to be absorbed without jeopardizing their host countries. They rely on the fickle kindness of strangers.

Any Universal Human Rights, based simply on a person being 'human', an inhabitant of the planet Earth, seems to be more of an abstract pipedream, created out of idle minds, perhaps with good intentions, but with no pragmatic, real-world experience - or, so the critics claim.

✺ *Historically, the only way a minority, of whatever kind, achieves or maintains power, is by the use of force.*

✹ *The very idea of democracy is that there is a distribution of power. This seems to be lost on some. No one has all the power, nor should they, in a democracy. Granted, some people, in practice, do seem to wield more power than others, and sometimes there is a corruption of this principle, but the principle still applies:* In a democracy, power has to be distributed for democracy to work.

✹ *Currently,* natural *rights as opposed to* national *rights seems to confer to people little in the way of safety or power. Any attempts to create an actualized Universal Human Rights* needs to have in its formulation a legal construct such that 'natural' rights have, within its structure, the force of law at least equal to* national *rights.*

✸ *Any Universal Human Rights imply that all people, with their individual, national, distinctiveness, must be 'reduced' to being merely human. Any public or political structure they may belong to does not take precedence over that fact.*

A person may lose or change their status in any particular group, but will always remain human. This fact makes each individual person their own political entity, giving them legal standing in any human sphere, and not relying on being part of any nation-state for protection, justification, or means of agency.

Of course, we have seen that the fate and status of many 'stateless' peoples all over the world, belies this statement. Basic universal human rights appear to be still an aspiration.

✸ *When a political party sees an actualized 'Big Brother' as a worthy goal to pursue and emulate, and does not hide this fact, this is telling on the host society.*

One reason some people fear and distrust certain immigrants is because they are so different. Additionally, these immigrants do not have deep roots or identification with their new country. In fact, they still seem to identify with their old country to such an extent that they resist, or refuse, assimilation.

Many having been in their new country for years, if not decades, yet they refuse to learn their new country's language. On many occasions they publicly fly their former county's national flag, again highlighting their 'foreignness' to native-born, and again, illustrating their unwillingness to fully assimilate.

This becomes even more problematic when they arrive in great numbers, seemingly posing a threat to the existing status quo.

Of course, a rational, functional, national immigration policy would help ameliorate this, but this is not happening as different political factions fight for supremacy, much as their constituents are doing in the streets.

🌞 *Many times, through no fault of their own, the rising number of stateless peoples residing within other State borders (they have no choice to do this as there is no 'unclaimed' land anywhere, anymore) comprise a perceived danger, that in past times may be likened to barbarians at the gate.*

🌞 *In a totalitarian State, when friend turns on friend, when family turns on family, the State's goals have been achieved. There is no longer any opposition to its rule. There is no longer any method, any capability, to oppose its rule.*

Totalitarian rule has achieved what some idealists had thought to be an ideal state, the complete individualization of peoples, and the society composed of them.

What is left is no one to turn to, no one to trust, no one to help or rely upon. What is left is a forced, default, loyalty to the State, as the State is all that is left.

✸ *The overall goal of the totalitarian regime is to instill an overall fear and distrust among the general population. This fear and distrust are not only about others in society, but about the individual person.*

The person no longer trusts their own thoughts, their own instincts, their own conclusions. The State, by proxy, becomes one giant confessional where the citizen, by virtue of their own internalized fear and distrust, confesses real or imaginary crimes to the State, seeking absolution and punishment.

✸ *The 'elite', however defined, do not trust the masses. Hence, the attraction for many of them to various forms of dictatorship, with them at the top, of course. They are the elite, after all.*

Trump's rise to power was and is legal, in that he used existing formal political and legal structure to attain the presidency. He continues to use formal legal structures, however corrupt they may sometimes be, to again rise to power. Despite his fame and recognition and support from some far-right people, it is the very current structure of the American social, political, and legal systems that allows him such prominence, such power. The American system is unbalanced. A new social, political, and legal contract needs to be created and established, otherwise, whether it is Trump or not, someone else will utilize these exiting flaws to game the system, and to again attempt to seize power.

It can be argued constantly about the totalitarian leader's thirst for power, and the lengths he will go to get it, but it must be remembered that such a leader derives his position from the support of the masses.

✹ *It has been recognized for many years, that wannabe dictators do not have to lie in order to convince people to support and vote for them. All they have to do is tell the truth, their proud truth, about their past sins, and what they will do once they have achieved power.*

There will be a significant segment of the population who will applaud this and support all that he says and wants to do.

Showing this segment of the population accurate facts and figures, accurate truths, ignores the fact that they do not care. They want what he wants.

✹ *Keep in mind, that once a totalitarian regime has gained power, there are no more innocent people - only party loyalists (if useful) and everyone else.*

People take on a utilitarian function. If they can serve the interests of the State, they have a use, and may live a little longer, at least till their usefulness ends.

✳ *The indifference, apathy, and even hostility, of the general masses to politics and government seems to characterize their viewpoint that these entities are not a factor in their lives, and that they do not want them to be so. That politics and government actually drain time, energy, and resources away from things that are truly 'real' in their daily lives of actual struggle. Basically, the masses do not want to be bothered.*

Then along comes someone with an answer. Someone who is willing to take on the burdensome tasks of governing. Who will handle all those tedious tasks the masses find so onerous and a waste of their valuable time, so that they can then continue with their own private affairs, undistracted, undisturbed.

Of course, eventually, they recognize that they do not live in isolation from that level and region of society where power resides, after all, just waiting for someone to grasp it, even just given to them.

Then as power, by its nature, must expand, the masses become part of its ever-increasing diet, forcing them to finally pay attention to the very thing they wanted to ignore.

✺ *The lust for power rises above race, economics, political stance, class, religion, above anything. Power, and the drive to possess it, becomes its own self-fulfilling prophecy, its own perpetual motion machine.*

Its attainment, its expansion, will only be limited by encountering an equal opposing force, or when it runs out of resource to exploit in its drive, when it exhausts itself, and everything around it.

✺ *When a political party's agenda does not consist of reasoned argument or debate, but rather draws on deep psychological issues prevalent in many people immune to logical persuasion, what we have left is the power of violence over conscience.*

⚛ *Is rule by democracy too much to ask of people? Election voter turnout remains low relative to potential voters. Voter understanding of the issues also remains problematic.*

Granted, issues of national and global import are complicated, but even the voter turnout for many local elections, where issues are relatively simpler, is low.

Democracy, the great experiment in self-rule, may have run its course, if people do not stand up for it. Work for it.

⚛ *The faceless masses, the marching morons, are the very fodder a wannabe dictator attracts and uses in the rise to power. However, it is this very anonymity that, unbeknownst to them, makes them so disposable.*

✺ *The fact that many of Trump's followers seem to have a basic contempt for common sense is perhaps an exaggeration. Sure, they ignore, some even praise, his flaws in personality, his crimes, his apparent moral and mental defects, but what they see and support is a person who exhibits all the traits and flaws they find in themselves. They bow before a mirror.*

✺ *Those who finally achieve power over the State, know that this seizure is only the beginning. There is no end. The continuation of power requires that the 'struggle' continues till it is embedded in every citizen, then in every new-born citizen, till there is no other thought in anyone but to engage in the constant struggle. The people become an integral part of the power structure, but have no actual individual power.*

✳ *Let us be honest, some people crave, yearn for violence, for the need to unleash their pent-up emotions, hatreds, resentments, fears.*

They just need an excuse, a direction, and permission. They get that permission from joining a group of like-minded people, and finding a cause and leader who sees their specialness and potential, and says: 'Yes, it is okay, you are okay, you are special, you have value, we need you, our people need you, our country needs you, I need you! Join me, join our crusade, protect our people, our way of life. Kick and stomp if you have to. Shoot and kill if you want to. For our cause is just and you are our new holy warriors!'

This, or something akin to it, they are told and believe. The blind marching morons of a lost cause that never really existed, but a useful tool for some.

✳ *Look to the people a wannabe dictator, or one who has already achieved power, has in his inner circle. This is telling of how he thinks and what kind of information and thought is being funneled his way.*

✺ *To be recognized and not forgotten is the goal of many in life. But the angry, the isolated, the socially desperate and excluded, want more. They want payback.*

Any 'movement' that offers this as an option against a society that offends and rejects them has their attention, and perhaps devotion. A place for their misplaced, displaced love. If violence is required, all the better. Violence allows them to stand out. It allows them to make a mark on a society that previously dismissed them as useless nonentities.

✺ *There is a sense before a storm, when some people recognize the gathering of clouds, that certain charge in the air, that feeling that some hurried action must be taken. There is an overwhelming feeling of fight or flight.*

⚙ *People talk about the banality of everyday life. Of its sameness, of the daily drudgery that manifests without joy, and of the soul-destroying purposelessness of it.*

This state of being however, is only achieved in a stable society, where there is no war or famine, or other disasters that make life 'interesting'.

Stability then, can be seen as simply soul destroying or as an opportunity, a platform, to achieve something greater, whom few in history have had a chance to experience.

⚙ *To break the bounds of society, to proclaim a personal self-sufficiency or morals and virtue all your own, is to reject everything and everyone.*

This illusion of power and freedom is just that, an illusion. Going through life inflicting harm and calling it freedom just makes you a lazy intellectual and a sociopath.

⊛ *Some people applaud Trump, not necessarily because they believe him or agree with him, but because of their perception that he is unmasking what they see as hypocrisy, of him saying and doing things that deep down some feel they want to say or do, at least for the moment, but would not be able to get away with.*

Hearing it said out loud, hearing the gasps of horror and shock such pronouncement have on the general population, seeing the consternation and confusion as normal people, including the media, have no idea how to respond, are all seen as positives. Thinking deeply about what he actually says and the implications, is not a factor.

⊛ *In the United States, there is a perception among many that political institutions and politicians exist only to serve certain elite people and private business interests, powerful corporations. Any common good done is an accidental byproduct; or, sometimes, only a concession to public pressure.*

✺ *The success of the MAGA-Right depends on the collapse of the system that allowed them to gain power in the first place.*

In fact, for them to win, the current system must be destroyed. They see everyone else as an enemy, one to be put down with a system that stands in the way of their paradise on Earth. God is on their side; they can do no wrong in achieving their goals.

These are the true believers. Other MAGA are just predatory assholes looking for power for its own sake.

✺ *Free thought, different thought, are not tolerated by totalitarian regimes. There is no distinction between private and public thought. Both are one and the same with the One Party. Differences are understood as deviances, and are seen as targets for elimination.*

✸ *It has long been noticed, that in tyranny's rise to power, the use of propaganda alone is not enough. Soon is seen a rise in violence as an attempt is made to couple propaganda and violence into a unified tool for control and oppression. Once power is clearly established, propaganda morphs into indoctrination. Violence never goes away.*

✸ *For some, their belief in the Universal Laws of Nature, demands that in a universe of death and destruction, a rule by tooth and claw, beast against beast, man against man, there is no room for quarter or compromise.*

Only the strong and righteous will prevail, and deserve to do so. Power is automatically bequeathed to the winner by means of a universe who's laws they are just obeying. They are but law-abiding citizen-soldiers. A social Darwinism in the extreme.

✺ *In a democratically governed country, the general background is composed of a silent majority who have no interest or understanding of how their government works.*

Most political campaigns fall on deaf, disinterested ears. If they think of government at all, it is almost as another aspect of nature, usually a negative one, a natural force they have no control over, but perhaps like rain, they can use a metaphorical umbrella in times of need, to offset happenings they almost equate to acts of God.

✺ *The disasters of Trump's business and private life are not seen as negatives to his MAGA supporters, just further evidence that he is one of them.*

✸ *The forever wars the United States has embroiled itself in over the past few decades has produced a deep cadre of combat veterans, now in civilian life.*

The experiences of the front lines in strange lands, with the need for total reliance on each other, the dangers and profound stress experienced, has produced contradictory effects. Some come back home and meld seamlessly back into society with little ripple.

Others, come back with symptoms of PTSD. But in this case, it is not the stress of prior combat that they exhibit, but the stress of trying to fit into what seems to them to be a meaningless existence.

A daily civilian routine of misery, fakeness, resentment, a perplexity of nonsense and lack of respect. Of being lost and alone in a society where they no longer have a place. The strain and yearning for the clarity, passion, and authenticity of combat, with brothers of the spear, taking its daily toll.

What we are left with are people who are ripe for recruitment by someone who promises the excitements, the regaining of lost respect, membership in a new tribe, the escape from the utter banality of civilian life, and, contradictorily, both the anonymity of being a simple grunt in renewed almost spiritual combat, with the feeling of individual accomplishment being a part of an historical movement. Of slaying the dragon one more time.

Of course, the new great leader (they are always 'great') understand all this and uses it to his own advantage. So, this mass of leaderless, rudderless veterans is given a new purpose, a new direction, and like many before them in history, will just end up in its historical ash-heap, perceived as mere pawns, forgotten, disposed, and dismissed, once again, with little gain.

A misused, abused, angry group of combat veterans, ready for a leader, any leader, who will summon them once again, to a new great cause. Wannabe heroes for a wannabe dictator. Who will mostly be remembered for the death and destruction caused, before history eventually rights itself.

✸ *Society in general does not have to break down for a populist leader to arise to power. All it takes is 'enough'. Enough disgruntled people who see no value in the current system for them. Enough who feel, and may actually be, excluded from the social, economic, or political structures of society. Enough who see no hope for themselves or their 'kind' in the current status quo. Enough, just enough, to sway, to topple, what may have seemed such a stable society and structure. Just enough, when no one is paying attention.*

✸ *No longer clamouring at the gates, as a society we produce our own barbarians, many dressed in three-piece suits.*

✸ *Today humanity faces both outside threats and inside threats, but all are overlapping. Until the advent of the* Sixth Extinction *and* Climate Change, *humanity had reached a point where its greatest danger no longer rested outside its realm.*

While many still refuse to recognize current on-going vast species extinction and the role humanity plays it this, the same is also true with climate change, and the dire consequences facing humanity because of these events.

As the Sixth Extinction and Climate Change become more and more obvious in their effects, with each passing day, humanity compounds these threats by ignoring the inner threat that comes from itself.

This inner threat is humanity's growing distrust of science and expert opinion, basing their decisions instead on personal beliefs and prejudices, bubble-news, and in so-called leaders, seeking power by saying and doing what people want to hear and not on what they need to hear, or what the truth actually is.

This inner threat is also comprised of the rise of anti-democracy movements throughout the world. It has taken centuries for democracy to grow, develop, and take its place in how humans organize themselves into political coalitions, in order to rule themselves, and not be ruled by others, particularly some sort of 'elite'.

This is in jeopardy, as people seem to have reached a self-rule fatigue of some kind, unwilling to do the work of ruling themselves, but rather giving away this power to any 'strongman' who promises them that they will live the good life without doing the necessary mental and physical work themselves to get there.

As has been repeated often by many, power not used is power lost. People who refuse to recognize and use their power, will lose it to those who will take it and use it for their own selfish gains, all at the cost of the general good and of the actual future of humanity on this planet.

⚙ *The drive, the lust for power, though sometimes masked in high virtue, is surprising in the scope of its attractors, from the thug on the street, to Supreme Court justices. No one seems immune to trying to gain power and control by any means, even through corruption, violence, and the gun.*

⚙ It is my party (country?), right or wrong! *Variants of this have been used throughout history to justify almost anything.*

✵ *A free society must not control with a leash, but must also offer a social safety net to catch those who may falter and fall, at some time. For instance, many Americans are only one paycheck away from homelessness. Should they be abandoned?*

Some may criticize this as socialism, even communism, a Big Brother approach, taking away natural consequences that teach people resilience, make them stronger and smarter.

But there is a limit. A society that leaves people to die in the streets is not just or free, and only teaches and institutionalizes, despair.

✵ *The equality of freedom produces an inequality in practice that many do not understand and fight against, creating systems that attempt to compensate, that end up diminishing the very equality so long sought and fought for.*

❀ *It is difficult to understand the so-called unconstrained capitalist's view of how people and society should work. Simply put, the free market should underlie all economic, and hence, political actions. Markets should, and will, find their own level. The hand of fallible man should leave free markets alone to find their natural level. Fallible man's interference will only make thigs worse, or even cause the very things they are trying to prevent by their trying to control things and events they cannot possible fully understand.*

Apparently, the idea, as represented by William Godwin, that best expressed and supported this view is that 'intention' to benefit others is the essence of virtue that leads to human happiness. Interesting, but also a deeply flawed position. Adam Smith's 'invisible hand' oftentimes, smacks people down.

Both the constrained and unconstrained positions base their economic views on a biased and limited, hence, incorrect, understanding of human nature. The constrained view sees human nature as inherently unchanging and selfish, thus it needs systems and exterior controls in order to minimize any potential damage this 'Man' may cause in the pursuit of profit. The unconstrained view, of course, view believes the opposite. As mentioned, the unconstrained view sees 'Man' as inherently good intentioned, so if we all just get out of the way, these good intentions will bear fruit, to the benefit of all.

Neither side actually captures the full complexity of human nature. Humans are capable of both selfishness and unselfishness, of working with others to benefit the group, and also of being a total bastard, thinking only of oneself. Sometimes, that same person can do both in a lifetime.

What is particularly irksome is when the unconstrained folks label the constrained folks as 'socialists' and themselves as, what, the heroes of laissez-faire *capitalism?*

Socialism, like Capitalism, we all know, comes in different flavours, the extremes of either are not good. Some fear that socialism will slide, inevitably, into Communism*. This is not necessarily true.*

Historically, we have all seen what laissez-faire *capitalism did to people and to the American economy. What is needed is an operating economic and political philosophy that captures and utilizes both viewpoints, capturing the full true complexity of* 'Man'.

Despite the clamouring of far-right voices, throwing out accusations of socialist or communist against their rivals, the current threat to our democracy is not some sort of centralized control and planning of the State over everyday citizens, but just the opposite, a complete decentralization of political and economic forces, with no guardrails to protect the country and the people from unscrupulous businesses, organizations, and powerful individuals. The Ayn Rand true believers, delude themselves with the 'great man' *hypothesis of history and economics. All one has to do is look to actual history to disprove such beliefs.*

⚙ *Just as we need guardrails on socialism, we also need guardrails on capitalism. In fact, any type of government needs guardrails.*

⚙ *The very idea of 'planning' in a State economy is seen as meddling, or even worse, a slid into socialism, then, further, inevitably into totalitarianism. This is, of course, nonsense.*

People plan, businesses plan, the capacity to plan is one of humanity's greatest gifts. Governments also have to plan.

But there is a big difference between a 'planned economy', ignoring market forces, for the State's idea and version of wisdom, and making some judicial planning on the use of government resources, based on the perceived happenings in the world.

Another difference is that good State planning does not assume that the Plan is always correct, or that it cannot be changed, or that there is only one source of input. Or, that there is only one Plan. The State projects into the future, certainly in the relative short-term, as part of its responsibility, and directs resources accordingly. Nothing nefarious. Nothing sinister. Not ignoring market forces, just a sometime small contributor to the process.

Sure, sometimes a government attempts to steer the economy a certain way – avoiding inflation, for instance. Sometimes, it gets it right, sometimes not.

This is a big difference from the fearsome 'planned economy' of communist countries. Even they now understand how futile such comprehensive, forced State planning was and is.

❂ *It is so easily forgotten sometimes, but in a democracy, the people are the State.*

☀ *Money, rather as seen as the root of all evil, should be seen as the great liberator of all people. Money is the token, this universal token, once earned, that allows anyone, if they want to, to be free from the land, free from property, and burdensome, restrictive possessions, that allows anyone to go where they please, to buy what they want, to live as money allows. While money can accumulate, creating hotspots, in general, money distributes power.*

☀ *The denial of intellectual and academic thought, the suppression of free and open debate, the redefining of the word 'liberty' to mean whatever is convenient, are clear and evident indications of a society's budding romance with totalitarian thought and action.*

While the majority of the people may not agree with this debasement of the social and intellectual climate, there is a significant number of like-minded people who do, and are willing to surrender what moral and intellectual capacity that they may have, to follow a leader who promises to return that which they most lack, self-respect, and a way to win it back, by whatever means necessary, from those whom they think are holding them back and down, and perverting their way of life.

For some, this yearning for violence can only be satisfied by actual violence. All they need is for someone to point the way.

⚘ *In relatively recent past times, the expressed biggest difference between the Republican and Democratic parties was their definition of and use of the size of the government. The Republicans prided themselves on demanding 'small' government, at the same time deriding the Democratic party as a party of 'large' government.*

Such descriptors, even if agreed upon by both parties, is wrong. It is a fight over language, only. It is a difference only in degree not kind. The debate, the difference, is just about how and where to spend, utilize, government resources.

Granted, the Democratic party tends to see the government as having a larger role in certain aspects of society, of seeing itself as a possible solution to problems that its resources could help with, that individuals could not accomplish on their own.

Republicans might not agree with this 'interference', but it is all just a matter of degree. Both sides are operating on the same spectrum, just starting at opposite ends. But it is a sliding scale, each side advancing and retreating as needs and viewpoints change.

This difference of opinion can then be discussed, can be adjudicated, can be compromised with. It does not turn each side automatically into an enemy. Such is not the case today. The demonization of each side hinders discussion and compromise, the very things that a democracy is based upon.

These are the indications to look for in deciding, as a citizen, as a voter, who you should listen to and support. In a democracy not everyone gets all that they want. Each side gets enough to continue. If some side gets everything that they want all the time, then it is not a democracy anymore.

In totalitarian regimes, if you are not a True Believer, you are automatically a disbeliever. And disbelievers are not tolerated.

For some, freedom is just too much. Too many choices, too much responsibility, too much accountability, too much risk. just too, too much.

They yearn for safety, for limited choice, for clear direction from someone who knows, for help in what to say and do, in how and what to think.

They will gladly give up chaotic freedom, and say thank you and please to those who take it away. Their 'future shock' is now, and they do not like it.

Many wonder at the support of Trump and his ilk. How could rational people see him, listen to him, and still support him. But as Friedrich A. Hayek pointed out: 'Intelligent people will tend to overvalue intelligence.'

So, Trump and his popularity amongst a certain segment of the population, should be understood from a position other than one of pure intellectual analysis.

It has been noticed by many that people in a free society become less and less able to distinguish the meaning of freedom and what it means to be free. Many man-in-the-street interviews have shown people's lack of understanding of the principles upon which their free society is based. And a certain misguided willingness to curb elementary freedoms, confusing some basic principles of freedoms with some outlandish form of anarchy. Granted, these types of interviews are not strictly scientific, but their consistency is telling.

This raises the question: Is freedom understood and appreciated only when it is lost? *Perhaps, but such an appreciation is not even possible if the people do not actually understand the word or concept, and grasp how it apples to their everyday lives.*

And it must be understood that there is always a segment of the population that actually prefers the 'dependability' *a dictatorship presents. Some of Russia's older generation say that they miss Stalin and the* 'stability' *he offered.*

✻ *Totalitarian regimes do not follow the dictates of market economics, nor do they follow the traditional logic of human welfare.*

They follow their own 'infallible' ideology, whatever it is, wherever it may lead. From mass burn pits, to concentration camps, to war, to mass starvation, to genocide, to complete and total subjugation by whatever means necessary.

Their ultimate goal is their holy grail, their only raison d'etre. Other people are only tools to get there, or hinderance to be removed.

✻ *The equality of freedom produces an inequality that many do not understand and fight against, creating systems that attempt to compensate, that end up diminishing the very equality so long sought and fought for.*

❂ *It will be noticed how much propaganda is utilized by people who are trying to convince others that their way is the best way, the one and only way to get what you want done.*

This is accomplished using mostly lies, half-truths, 'star' speakers, taking actual facts out of context; basically, a myriad number of methods to convince people that they are right and the other side is not only wrong, but evil.

One telling point is that they never apologize for their speech and actions. That would show weakness and fallibility.

Unfortunately, such propaganda is just the beginning. Once they are in power, propaganda is no longer needed, except perhaps to an outside world. Now two other methods become their preferred modus operandi: indoctrination and terror.

❂ *The history of the future is written in the past - usually in blood.*

✹ *The gulf between reality and fiction, is for some, much too large to jump. So, they remain stranded on fiction's shores, while reality slowly recedes from their vision.*

✹ *Deluded Republican voters are not convinced by facts. They seem to admire the mysterious, the sinister, the conspiracy, the secrets behind the curtain, even if those secrets do not exist. These hold more sway in their minds than any proven fact ever could. The savvy Republicans, the power brokers, the ones pulling the curtain strings, just ignore inconvenient facts, truth immaterial to their pursuit of power.*

✵ *Currently, the far-right in the United States has a tendency to speak in absolutes.*

In the past, as Western societies were developing, and moving away from a total reliance on religion for authority, especially post-Renaissance, this absoluteness was now replaced with using the budding knowledge base and influence of the growing understanding of science.

Especially, an attempt was made to converge science, or actually pseudoscience, and religion into a unified argument supporting their various claims.

Today, as the far-right has foresworn science, they are left with only religion as the ultimate foundation for their position.

They are only following God's will, etc. But they are still absolutists, disregarding political and social pragmatism and compromise necessary in a working democracy.

Sometimes the 'overreach' of government in terms of perceived unnecessary laws, policies, regulations, rules, etc., is seen as a justification for some of pushing a far-right agenda of resistance, sometimes violent resistance, against such overreach.

Demanding a dismantling of the whole 'administrative state' system to allow some sort of* lessai faire *capitalism to flourish in its place, to have less government 'interference'. Some sort of Libertarianism* to replace it.*

A more prudent course of action would be to just attempt to repeal the offending laws, policies, or regulations. This is how things work in a democracy.

The world is now too complex, too integrated, to not see the nation and the rest of the world as one great system, each part affecting every other part. Nothing in isolation.

The difficulty with supply chains in the recent past pandemic underscores this very well.

No one government or person can see or understand this overall complexity, nor should they try to control it.

But some things as individuals and as a society we can and should do within our limited understanding and power.

If we get things wrong, as we will, we need to understand and utilize the processes of and for change we have created in our democratic institutions.

For the current Republican party success is defined as the furtherance of the Lie. However, this Lie can change. But the change does not matter, as eventually the Republican base will believe anything told to them.

✹ *Political parties, separated by principle, must still find a way to govern the State when either one gains power.*

The simple necessities of government must still be carried out. The very people they demonize on the campaign trail are now their constituents. Are now their colleagues.

A common ground must be established, otherwise effective governance will be impossible.

POWER
&
STATE

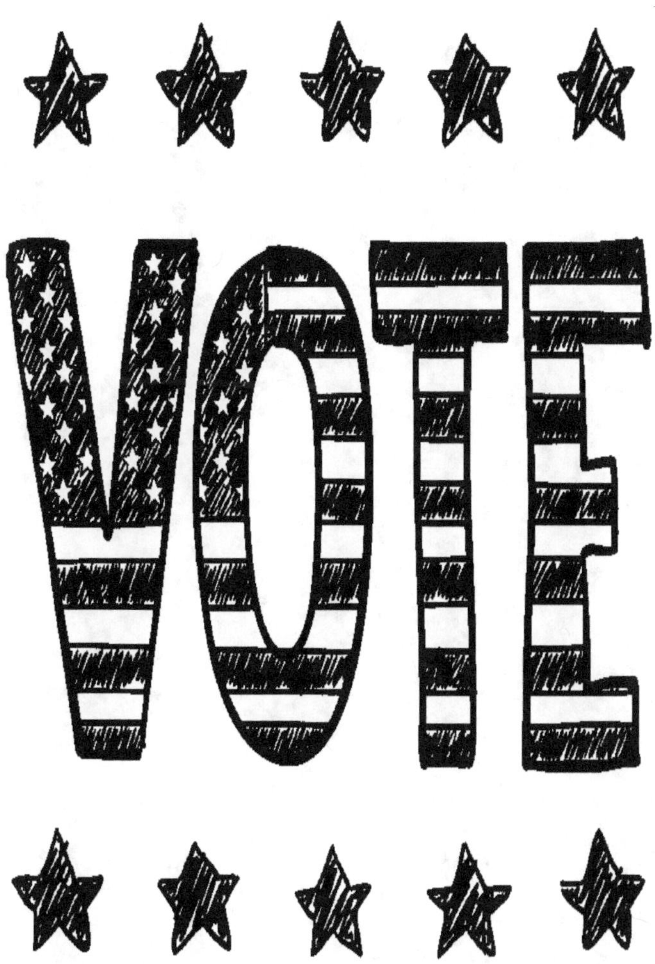
VOTE

UNIVERSAL HUMAN RIGHTS & DUTIES

The following UNIVERSAL HUMAN RIGHTS & DUTIES is an attempt to create and formulate a consensual, yet, necessarily simple in format, charter, that can be applied across a wide variety of dispersed, non-homogenized, Human nations, societies, cultures, and peoples.

At this point in time, this charter is more a fantasy than a reality, yet considering the current world situation with rampant war, famines, widespread diseases, increasing mass migrations, and the looming threat of climate change, it was felt that an attempt to formulate something simple, yet doable (?), is not only needed, necessary, but crucial to the actual survival of our global civilization, if not our species.

Many sources, and authors (including Professor Nalangu, who is a contributing author to this project), were used to create this charter. Some sources are listed at the end, but in particular: A SYSTEMATIC THEORY OF UNIVERSAL ETHICS AND A CODE FOR GLOBAL MORAL EDUCATION, by Enno A. Winkler MD PhD (2022), was used as a framework. It is simple in structure, yet captures what needs to be said and done. The simplicity may rest in that it had a single author, and was not written by a committee.

We all hope that in reading this, you can find something that resonates within you, and can motivate you to promote this, or something akin to it, to your respective political representatives.

It is recognized that this manifesto is incomplete, particularly in the ENFORCEMENT section, as is common in many of the listed sources; for example, in the Geneva Conventions on the Rules of Engagement in war.

UNIVERSAL HUMAN RIGHTS & DUTIES
Guiding Principles

This UNIVERSAL HUMAN RIGHTS & DUTIES is an attempt to create and formulate a consensual, yet, necessarily simple in format, charter, that can be applied across a wide variety of dispersed, non-homogenized, Human nations, societies, cultures, and peoples.

Human caused extinction may be avoided if Humanity will be willing to accept basic rules of common conduct.

UNIVERSAL HUMAN RIGHTS & DUTIES binds all people collectively and each one separately.

Commandments

(1) Respect the other as yourself.
(2) Respect the truth.
(3) Do not steal.
(4) Respect life.
(5) Protect nature.

<u>Principles</u>

1) Each human being is endowed with personal dignity (dignity is the right of a person to be valued and respected for their own sake, and to be treated ethically. The Golden Rule, the Rule of Reciprocity, or Kant's Categorical Imperative, come to mind as basic examples).

2) An individual's liberty finds its limits where the dignity of the other begins.

3) State, religious, economic, and other office holders are in service to the individual.

4) Human aspirations for progress can only be realized by agreed values and standards applying to all people and institutions at all times.

5) The rational actor model, must cease being the basis for political and social policy. Making the various populations feel like they belong to the greater group, may be the single best long-term strategy for reducing conflict and war: building cohesive societies stops both internal violence and intergroup conflict.

6) The antidote to polarization comes from overlapping group membership and loyalties.

7) Policies that distribute the pie more widely should lead to more balanced power in society, and edge societies towards peace.

8) Peace is not just an absence of war. It is a positive activity. Active peace can be defined as the availability or provision of food, shelter, health, education, and justice, as well as freedom and human dignity. If these things can be provided for, or made available, to all and any peoples, then war, itself, becomes the outlier, not the expected norm. Governments, nations, peoples, should be looking at their own societies to see where they fall short on these attributes of active peace, and fill the gaps where needed. They then should also look outside their own borders to promote an active peace in those societies that lack this foundation. *It will be discovered that a truly comprehensive active peace cannot be found anywhere if it is lacking somewhere.* Peace is not just a given. Peace cannot be assumed to be the base state for all humans, forever. Peace must be pursued and fought for, on many fronts. This is not an oxymoron; it is a basic truth.

9) The freedom of indifference is not acceptable to a humane, progressive society. History has repeatedly warned that freedom without involvement and acceptance of responsibility can destroy the freedom itself; whereas, when rights and responsibilities are balanced, then freedom is enhanced and a better world can be created.

10) When power is unequal, unaccountable, and centralized, a society is left vulnerable to the whims and private interests of rulers and elites. This must be recognized and accounted for.

11) The more freedom we enjoy, as a society and as individuals, the greater the responsibility we bare, toward others as well as ourselves.

12) We have a duty and responsibility to protect and promote a safe, stable and healthy environment, promoting respect, protection, and preservation of the uniqueness and diversity of all forms of life. To promote an adequate use of resources avoiding excessive exploitation and consumption.

13) Sovereignty is not absolute. In a recognized *'league of nations'*, full sovereignty is recognized as not being absolute. Certain rights, duties, obligations are seen as *'international'* in scope. In a Democracy, if all Rights devolve to the individual, the individual must then have a means to protect those Rights if the Law cannot or refuses to do so, otherwise those Rights become meaningless.

14) Many people have asked, and many governments, and organizations, have disputed us on this issue, but the question is: *Why is so much emphasis placed on the individual?* The reason is that, if you look

closely at the prior Principles, it will be noticed that most mention and require that the individual is crucial and central to the accomplishment of the Human Rights & Duties listed. Our perspective is that the individual is the foundation upon which all societies depend and function. Nothing would exist without the individual. This journey, this search, for a principled, coherent, just society, begins and ends with the individual; hence, the individual's importance in this schema.

Enforcement

The violation of these principles and commandments is subject to social rejection and punishment under equal rules and laws for everyone.

The importance of the concept of self-responsibility towards attaining the self-realization of these listed *Principles* cannot be overlooked or overstated. Unless each individual is involved in the creation, accomplishment is diminished, or even may be impossible, certainly more difficult.

This section is based, in part, on:

The Magna Carta (1215)

The United States of America's Declaration of
Independence (1776)

The United States Constitution (1787)

France's Declaration of the Rights of Man
and of the Citizen (1789)

THE UNIVERSAL DECLARATION OF
HUMAN RIGHTS (1948)

UNIVERSAL DECLARATION OF HUMAN
RESPONSIBILITIES (1997)

EARTH CHARTER (2000)

MILLENIUM DEVELOPMENT GOALS (2000)

RESPONSIBILITY TO PROTECT (2005)

THE 2030 AGENDA FOR SUSTAINABLE
DEVELOPMENT (2015)

A SYSTEMATIC THEORY OF UNIVERSAL
ETHICS AND A CODE FOR GLOBAL MORAL
EDUCATION
By Enno A. Winkler MD PhD (2022)

(All worthwhile reads.)

The great enemy of freedom is the alignment
of political power with wealth.
~ Wendell Berry

Religion is regarded by the common people
as true, by the wise as false, and by
rulers as useful
~ Seneca

We know that no one ever seizes power
with the intention of relinquishing it.
~ George Orwell

Power lacks morals or principles. It only has interests.
~ Horacio Castellanos Moya

The sources of power are many. Which source is chosen,
illuminates a person's nature.
~ Santiago Bardo

Power is dangerous. It corrupts the best
and attracts the worst.
~ Ragnar Lothbrok

The greater the power, the more dangerous the abuse.
~ Edmund Burke

It doesn't matter where you stand,
but rather what you stand for.
~ Mathieson Street

Democracy is a process.
~ Elizabeth Rutherglen

All political power is a trust.
~ Charles James Fox

STUFF

Lucy Nalangu Bio.

Teacher, writer, social activist, social scientist, political philosopher, formerly Professor of Law, History & Moral Philosophy at the University of Nairobi, previously taught at the University of Oxford, UK, and Harvard University, US. Currently, is a freelance researcher, professional writer, commentator, and consultant.

James Sawers Bio.

James Sawers is a citizen of the United States of America, having emigrated from the United Kingdom at an early age. He has a bachelor's degree in psychology, and a master's in management. He is a sandan in the Japanese martial art of aikido.

He is also a veteran, a former paratrooper with the 82nd Airborne Division (*All the Way!*): 2/504 (*Devils in Baggy Pants*) & 2/508 (*Death from Above*). A former member of the 2nd Infantry Division (Indianhead) (*Second to None!*) - ROK/U.S. Combined Division; 2nd Battalion, 9th Infantry Regiment (Mechanized) (*Keep Up the Fire!)* "Manchu" (Imjin Scouts).

Definitions

<u>Moral Philosophy</u>

<u>Character List</u>

<u>Nation, Nation-State, State,
Sovereign State,
Country</u>

<u>Socialism</u>

<u>Communism</u>

<u>Democratic Socialism</u>

<u>Democracy</u>

<u>Liberalism</u>

<u>Libertarianism</u>

<u>Administrative State</u>

Moral Philosophy

Moral philosophy is the branch of philosophy that contemplates what is right and wrong. It explores the nature of morality and examines how people should live their lives in relation to others.

Moral philosophy has three branches.

One branch, meta-ethics, investigates big picture questions such as, "What is morality?" "What is justice?" "Is there truth?" and "How can I justify my beliefs as better than conflicting beliefs held by others?"

Another branch of moral philosophy is normative ethics. It answers the question of what we ought to do. Normative ethics focuses on providing a framework for deciding what is right and wrong. Three common frameworks are deontology, utilitarianism, and virtue ethics.

The last branch is applied ethics. It addresses specific, practical issues of moral importance such as war and capital punishment. Applied ethics also tackles specific moral challenges that people face daily, such as whether they should lie to help a friend or co-worker.

(Wikipedia)

Character List

For simplicities sake, particular definitions used in this book parallel, and are guided by, those of Hannah Arendt, from her book: *The Origins of Totalitarianism*, However, any changes, deviations, are this author's *'mistakes'*.

The People

The *People* are the citizens of a nation-state. They are the people who work. They form the body politic and are the ultimate source of authority in the functioning nation-state. They are often mistaken for the Mob or the Masses, both of which are degenerations of the People. In the mid-19th century, the People get split into classes, allowing for the Mob and the Masses to make their appearance.

The Mob

The *Mob* consists of the refuse of all classes of society. They search for a strong-man or great leader to follow. They always use extra-parliamentary (and often violent) means to accomplish political goals since they are not represented by parties that are based on the classes they have been ejected from. The Mob also plays a role in imperialism.

The Masses

The *Masses* refers to the mass of isolated, atomized individuals that is created by the destruction of the nation-state and the accumulation of capital during imperialism. The Masses are not the same as the Mob.

While the Mob is the refuse of all classes, the Masses are created by the apparent liquidation of classes. The Masses are the basis of totalitarian movements, which rely on a mass of humans who have lost all relations to their fellow man.

The Totalitarian Leader

The Totalitarian Leader is typified by Hitler and Stalin. The will of the Totalitarian Leader is the supreme law in a totalitarian regime, and all those who carry out this *supreme law* view themselves as merely instruments of the Leader's will and ideology rather than autonomous individuals making choices. The Totalitarian Leader is incredibly famous and charismatic, but will be forgotten immediately when he dies. Furthermore, he is the source of the *infallible predictions* so characteristic of totalitarian propaganda.

From: GradeSaver; Summary of *The Origins of Totalitarianism*, by Hannah Arendt; Character List.

Nation, Nation-State, State, Sovereign State, Country

Nation is a large body of people united by common origin, history, culture, ethnicity, or language. The main difference between *State* and *Nation* is that State is a political and legal entity whereas Nation is a socio-cultural entity. A State is a territory considered as an organized political community under one government.

A **State** is a territorial entity, with a permanent population, defined borders, and a government that effectively controls the territory. States in which the overwhelming majority of people belong to one nation are known as **Nation-States.**

State, Nation, and *Country* are all terms that describe groups of people who live in the same place and have a great deal in common. But while **States** and **Sovereign States** are political entities, **Nations** and **Countries** might or might not be. A **Sovereign State** (sometimes called an Independent State) has the following qualities:

1. A **State** is a territory with its own institutions and populations.
2. A **Nation** is a large group of people who inhabit a specific territory and are connected by history, culture, or another commonality.
   Nation is also a large body of people united by common origin, history, culture, ethnicity, or language. The main difference between **State** and **Nation** is that State is a political and legal entity

whereas Nation is a socio-cultural entity. A State is a territory considered as an organized political community under one government.

3. A **Nation-State** is a cultural group (a Nation) that is also a State (and may, in addition, be a **Sovereign State).**

4. The word **Country** can be used to mean the same thing as **State, Sovereign State**, or **Nation-State**. It can also be used in a less political manner to refer to a region or cultural area that has no governmental status. Examples include Wine Country (the grape-growing area of northern California) and Coal Country (the coal-mining region of Pennsylvania).

5. A **Sovereign State** is a state with its own institutions and populations that has a permanent population, territory, and government. It must also have the right and capacity to make treaties and other agreements with other States.

A **Sovereign State** (sometimes called an Independent State) also has the following qualities:

a) Space or territory that has internationally recognized boundaries

b) People who live there on an ongoing basis

c) Regulations governing foreign and domestic trade

d) The ability to issue legal tender that is recognized across boundaries

e) An internationally recognized government that provides public services and police power and has the right to make treaties, wage war, and take other actions on behalf of its people

f) Sovereignty, meaning that no other State should have power over the country's territory

~ Wikipedia; Various Sources

Socialism, Communism
Democratic Socialism, Democracy,
Liberalism, Libertarianism,
Administrative State

<u>SOCIALISM</u>: The meaning of SOCIALISM is any of various egalitarian economic and political theories or movements advocating collective or governmental ownership and administration of the means of production and distribution of goods. Some people see socialism (in Marxist theory) as a transitional social state between the overthrow of capitalism and the realization of Communism.

<u>COMMUNISM</u>: Communism is a form of government most closely associated with the ideas of Karl Marx, which he outlined in The Communist Manifesto. Communism is based on the goal of eliminating socioeconomic class struggles by creating a classless society in which everyone shares the benefits of labor and the state controls all property and wealth.

<u>DEMOCRATIC SOCIALISM</u>: A political ideology that supports the establishment of a democratically run and decentralized form of socialist economy. Modern democratic socialists vary widely in their views of how a proper socialist economy should function, but all share the goal of abolishing capitalism. Democratic socialism is a variant of socialism where the government is organized by democracy. In short, it believes that social and economic decisions should be made by those whom they most affect. The combination of the two ideologies of democracy and

socialism makes democratic socialism. Democratic socialists believe that both the economy and society should be run democratically—to meet public needs, not to make profits for a few. To achieve a more just society, many structures of the government and economy must be radically transformed through greater economic and social democracy so that ordinary citizens can participate in the many decisions that affect their lives. Democratic socialists do not want to create an all-powerful government bureaucracy, but at the same time do not want big corporate bureaucracies to control our society either.

<u>DEMOCRACY</u>: is a system of government in which state power is vested in the people or the general population of a state. Under a minimalist definition of democracy, rulers are elected through competitive elections while more expansive definitions link democracy to guarantees of civil liberties and human rights in addition to competitive elections. In a direct democracy, the people have the direct authority to deliberate and decide legislation. In a representative democracy, the people choose governing officials through elections to do so.

<u>LIBERALISM:</u> Is a political and moral philosophy based on the rights of the individual, liberty, consent of the governed, political equality, right to private property and equality before the law. Liberals espouse various and often mutually warring views depending on their understanding of these principles but generally support private property, market economies, individual rights (including civil rights and human rights), liberal democracy, secularism, rule of law, economic and political freedom, freedom of speech, freedom of the press, freedom of assembly, and freedom of religion, constitutional government and privacy rights.

Liberalism is frequently cited as the dominant ideology of modern history.

LIBERTARIANISM: Libertarianism, is a political philosophy that takes individual liberty to be the primary political value. A political philosophy that advocates only minimal state intervention in the free market and the private lives of citizens. It may be understood as a form of liberalism, classical liberalism in particular, the political philosophy associated with the English philosophers John Locke and John Stuart Mill, the Scottish economist Adam Smith, and the American statesman Thomas Jefferson. Liberalism seeks to define and justify the legitimate powers of government in terms of certain natural or God-given individual rights. These rights include the rights to life, liberty, private property, freedom of speech and association, freedom of worship, government by consent, equality under the law, and moral autonomy (the ability to pursue one's own conception of happiness, or the 'good life'). The purpose of government, according to liberals, is to protect these and other individual rights, and in general liberals have contended that government power should be limited to that which is necessary to accomplish this task. Libertarians are classical liberals who strongly emphasize the individual right to liberty. They contend that the scope and powers of government should be constrained so as to allow each individual as much freedom of action as is consistent with a like freedom for everyone else. Thus, they believe that individuals should be free to behave and to dispose of their property as they see fit, provided that their actions do not infringe on the equal freedom of others.

ADMINISTRATIVE STATE: is a term used to describe the power that some government agencies have to write, judge, and enforce their own laws. Since it pertains to the structure and function of government, it is a frequent topic in political science, constitutional law, and public administration. The administrative state is created when legislative (law-making) bodies, like the U.S. Congress or the U.K. Parliament, delegate their lawmaking powers to administrative or private entities, as in other government agencies, like the United States' EPA, for example. In recent years, in the U.S., some argue that the Administrative State runs counter to the U.S. Constitution. Some recent court cases reflect this argument. Some think that if the power of the Administrative State is cut down or severely diminished, the government will become paralyzed and will be unable to function effectively. Laws made by administrative agencies are typically distinguished from laws written by the legislature, and given a separate term like 'regulations' or 'rules', or referred to in codified form as 'codes'.

~ Wikipedia; Various Sources

Veterans Crisis Hotline

VETERANS CRISIS HOTLINE

We're here anytime, day or night – 24/7

If you are a Veteran in crisis or concerned about one, connect with our caring, qualified responders for confidential help. Many of them are Veterans themselves.

- Call **988 and select 1**
- Text **838255**
- https://www.veteranscrisisline.net/get-help-now/chat/
- Call TTY if you have hearing loss
  - **800-799-4889**

or:
1-800-273-8255 and Press 1

Social Media Contact

If you want to hear more about James Sawers's upcoming books and works, or contact him, or join him on social media:

Facebook:

James Sawers
www.facebook.com/sawersX

Email: nothingwerks42@gmail.com

(The above methods are the ONLY
way to contact the author.)